Lawrence & Jonah
Simon & Mia —

How Beautiful!

& Maybe you'll all enjoy
The Boston Children's Museum
together, where flies
book was once the
shared by the
author & A & Jo &
Your Grammat Stern

YOUR FAMILY
MY FAMILY

YOUR FAMILY

MY FAMILY

Written and illustrated by JOAN DRESCHER

To Kitty
It was fun to
ve at the children
museum today.
Thanks for all
your help!
Joan

WALKER AND COMPANY •New York, New York

To my mother and the family that was.
To Ken and the family that is.

Library of Congress Cataloging in Publication Data

Drescher, Joan E
  Your family, my family.

  SUMMARY: Briefly describes several kinds of
families and cites some of the strengths of family life.
  1. Family—Juvenile literature. [1. Family]
I. Title.
HQ734.D84   1980   306.8   79-9602
ISBN 0-8027-6382-0
ISBN 0-8027-6383-9 lib. bdg.

Text & Illustrations Copyright © 1980 by Joan Drescher

First published in the United States of America in 1980 by the Walker Publishing Company, Inc.
Published simultaneously in Canada by Beaverbooks, Ltd., Pickering, Ontario.

Trade. ISBN: 0-8027-6382-0   Reinf. ISBN: 0-8027-6383-9

Library of Congress Catalog Card Number 79-9602

Printed in the United States of America.

10 9 8 7 6 5 4 3 2 1

Families are made of mothers, fathers, sisters, brothers,
uncles, aunts, cousins, grandparents, and friends.
A family is people, living together, sharing, caring.

People are born into families,

adopted into families,

and some people just come together to make a family.

It doesn't matter if your family is big

or small, you are still a family.

A family can have two parents, or one, or none.
Grandparents can act as parents, so can foster parents.

Sara lives in an apartment in the city with her family.
Every morning, after she makes her bed, she goes to
a day-care center while her parents are at work.

Roger is adopted. Sometimes he wonders what his natural parents look like and sometimes, when he feels angry, he wishes he lived with them. But the mom and dad who adopted him love him, and he loves them—most of the time— and they need one another to be a family.

Kim's mother works, so Kim helps her dad with the house
and her baby sister. Some of her friends think it's funny
that her dad does all the cooking—until they taste his pizza!

Peter has two families. His parents are divorced and each
has married again. During the week he shops for his mom, and
on weekends he washes the car for his dad. Sometimes he shops
for his dad and washes the car for his mom.

Margo and Rita are Peggy's family. Although Margo is her real mother, Peggy feels as if she has two mothers.
That's twice as nice, except when they are both angry at her.

Tom lives with an extended family of many adults and children.
Sometimes there is a house meeting where feelings and ideas
are expressed. Tom said he was tired of setting the table,
so now his chore is watering the plants.

David lives with his grandparents. Grandma is the best cook in the world, and Grandpa knows the answer to everything. But sometimes David wishes they'd let him stay out as late as the other kids.

Lisa and her mother are a family all by themselves. Sometimes
when her mother is at work, Lisa gets lonely and calls her.
It's good to be close when you don't have a lot of people to love.

John and his sister, Jena, live in a foster home. They were separated once, and were very unhappy. They like their new home and parents and hope they'll never have to be apart again.

Sometimes you need to be with your family.

Sometimes you need to be by yourself.

Sharing is what makes a family work.

You can share your feelings with your family.

You can really be yourself with your family.

You can have a fight with someone in your family and get
very angry, but deep inside you know they still love you.
And you still love them.

People in a family care for one another.